Gathering

Seeds of Encouragement

Verna Bowman

Published by
Broken Shoe Press
Valley Forge PA 19481
www.lorihynson.com

Edited by Christy Distler

Cover Design, Interior image by
Kelly Vanek, Cassidy Communications, Inc

Interior illustrations by
Shannon Kehs

ISBN 978-0-9890790-3-7
Printed in the United States of America.

Scribing Scraps

Life is full and we're stuck for time. That's why it is important to seek a sacred space . . . for just a moment.

Gathering is a collection of writings taken from a blog created as an extension of ministry to hurting women, *Encouraging Women One Story at a Time.* It isn't a devotional, a journal, or a coloring book—but it can be a little of each, a quiet companion to come away and rest a while as you discover more of Him and more of you.

A daybreak therapy can be praying with a pen, recording trials of yesterday that have become blessings of today. I believe an important part of growing our faith is through journaling, simply scribing the scraps of life you wish to preserve.

Every day becomes another page in our life story, yet many things go unnoticed and disappear into the day. Our story may look like blank pages with unanswered questions, unless we allow God to write in the white space. As you reflect on the thought or question at the end of each writing, my hope is that you will gather your own pieces of encouragement.

Life is like a blowing dandelion; it blooms and clothes an entire landscape with color, then fades into pieces that scatter to the wind. *So, may we gather the pieces.*

And may His Word spread like wildflowers all over your heart,

Verna

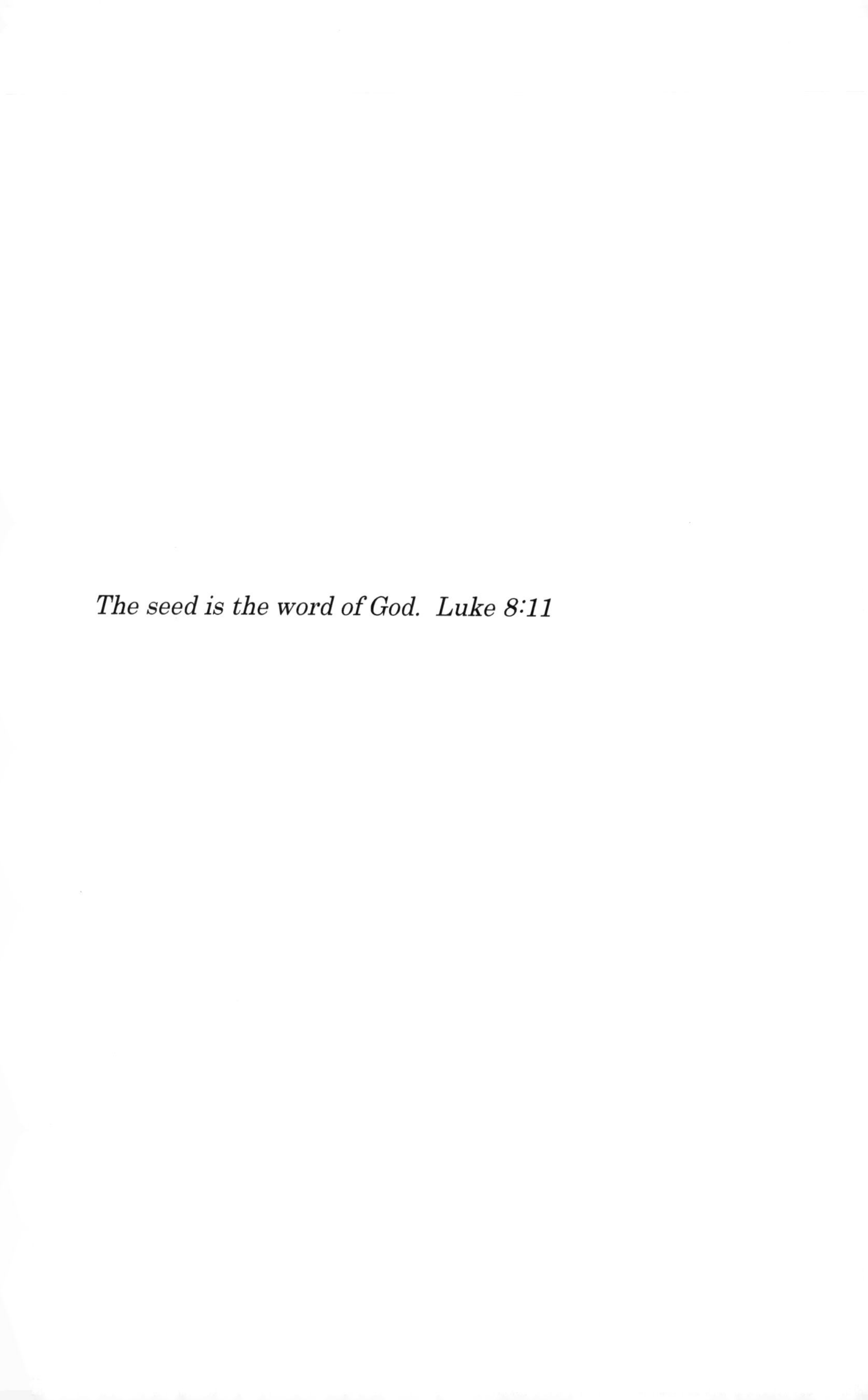

The seed is the word of God. Luke 8:11

Gathering . . .

Expectations

For she thought, "If I just touch His garments, I shall get well." Mark 5:28

How do you define an expectation—a hope too far out of reach? I recently had a conversation with a wise man who reminded me that hope and expectation are different, but actually the same.

So I looked both words up in the Greek and found the word *hope* means favorable and confident expectation. Sounds like faith. The word *expectation* means reaching out in readiness. Sounds like faith in action.

Right away, I thought of my favorite unnamed lady—she's right there in Mark 5. The woman who suffered chronic bleeding for twelve years had faith enough to reach out. The unnoticed one pressed in hard against the crowd surrounding Jesus so she could just touch the dusty edge of His holy garment. The beauty of her journey gave her an expectation driven by faith, and she believed if she could only get near enough to Jesus, she would be healed. So she reached out and believed. No boundaries.

And she was . . . and she received it . . . and she told about it.

What do we do with the unexpected, the unwanted—do we reach out and let it make us whole? Her wholeness came by waiting for a dozen years and reaching with trembling and confident expectation.

I think of what I've learned from another wise man, son-in-law Scott, the farmer. He doesn't waste sweat and seed for no harvest. He believes the effort will bear fruit. The plow is put to earth in expectation, not just hope. So both wise men helped me see the difference and similarity.

True hope in the Lord isn't a wish; it's a confident belief in an unlimited Father.

Of course, if we're not careful, our very human expectations can go wrong and let us down when we think we should have more, people should be more, and disappointing circumstances should be less. We're not always careful, and oh-so-human.

Have you ever expected someone to be just as you designed and they weren't? *Oh. you haven't?*

Maybe we need to lower our expectations to lower our disappointments, and reach out high to the One who doesn't let us down.

God delights in surprising us. Clear from Genesis to Revelation, that's how He shows up, from a garden to the clouds—and that's how He'll return. Unexpected.

Who are we that the Lord should notice and pour out unexpected blessings? His.

What is your expectation?

Woodstock to Wonderstruck

Therefore if any man is in Christ, he is a new creature; the old things passed away; behold new things have come. 2 Corinthians 5:17

Growing up in an age of innocence followed by one of the most violent decades in American history was a bitter mix. The '60s were a major turning point in the history of our country, when social upheaval dominated the landscape. Having one foot in the '50s and one in the '60s became a difficult path to walk.

Where were you when the world spun out of control?

I was there.

There is a time for all of us when the clock stopped with the unforgettable moments that changed our world. I've lived long enough to experience when the first man entered space, when President Kennedy was assassinated, and when Martin Luther King Jr. had a dream.

When there was no peace on earth, we left for the moon. And when there was no peace on my earth, I went to Max Yasgur's hog farm.

My world didn't make sense two score and five years ago, and as I'm writing this blog piece at the time of the forty-fifth anniversary of Woodstock, it still doesn't. So while some went to outer space, I went to a little piece of earth in Upstate New York to hide in the middle of a half million people dancing in the mud.

Looking back on the turbulent times of my world then and the one I live in now, *I wonder why* . . . why hundreds of thousands of young people congregating in a mud-drenched field—dealing with food shortages, unsanitary conditions, and torrential rain—didn't have so much as a fight break out. And why everyone helped one another.

Today we're at war with ourselves.

I believe everyone experiences their own Woodstock along the way as they look for what they can't find.

A few years ago I returned to what was once Yasgur's farm in Bethel. Strangely enough, the word *bethel* means sacred ground. While I was going my own way trying to outsmart Omnipotence, somehow God found me on my very crooked path.

While chasing music and futility, the faithful God of heaven was chasing me. Six sin-filled years after Woodstock, wallowing in muddy grace, I caught a glimpse of crumbs leading to Glory and my life changed forever. Struck with the wonder of an awesome God.

(*Crumbs Along the Broken Path, 2014*)

Do you believe that God can re-do you and forever change your life?

Everybody Has a Story

Your eyes saw my unformed substance; in your book were written, the days that were ordained for me, when as yet there was none of them. Psalm 139:16 ESV

We all have a story. It's already written. And don't we love hearing stories?

When I was a child, I loved listening to stories of long ago as my grandmother told it – weaving life into gold. It allowed me to see glimpses of her fleeting metamorphosis from a young girl to the wise and wrinkled on the pages of her story.

Stories were everywhere I listened. I'd go next door and hear old neighborhood men resting on porch rockers, whittling figures from dead wood, spinning yarns of what could have been . . . *if only*.

In the schoolroom, I'd hear historical tales of the founding heroes who walked the earth with feet of clay and wondered why their story wasn't perfect. And then I heard biblical stories of divine heroes and found the flawed and fallible hidden between the covers of Scripture. Their story wasn't perfect either. Gee, I didn't expect that.

And so Gramma, old gray whittlers, heroes who made it into history books and Bibles all had a story that told of . . . *if only*. Like mine. Everybody has a unique and valuable story whether written in a journal, a textbook, or a holy book.

And no one has the same one.

There's something healing about visiting your-own-deep-self and finding out what you're about. It's the secret place where we recognize moments we couldn't see without looking from an aerial view of our life through the Father's eyes.

If we dissect our experiences to discover who reigned, in spite of it all, we'll realize our timeline was carefully covered from birth to final breath. And ever-after.

The holy Author of nonfiction has handwritten a story designed just for you. And yet many of us would like to rewrite it. *I would.* We can choose to own or deny our story—to thrive or merely survive the chapters. But if we simply go through daily motions on a pretend journey in a land of what we wish, we'll never truly discover who He is or who we are, or the purpose behind it all.

As we walk this life by trial and error right alongside founding fathers and patriarchs, our great hope is that no matter how broken the path we've taken—it can be redeemed.

So, how do we change the way we *read* the story we wish were rewritten? Review the chapters that end in defeat and believe for a victorious sequel. We can believe the Word of God and begin right on the step we're on—the next one. It can take us to a new place no matter where we've visited or how long we stayed.

I've lived life long, and in that time I've learned there is a great story wrapped inside the one standing right in front of us. We just need to take the time to listen to their story and realize that sometimes that means listening between the words.

How do you read your unedited story? Do you wish you could rewrite it?

Chasing More

And you will seek Me and find Me, when you search for Me with all your heart. Jeremiah 29:13

Chasing dreams, possessions, and power seem to be the things we run after but never catch enough to satisfy. We chase what the world offers, the things that temporarily captivate. And oh-so-late we see it run through our wrinkled fingers.

And then we wish and wish again we had run after something we could actually hold onto.

David had a few dreams of his own and plenty of possessions, and experienced the power of a king, but the man after God's own heart continually chased after the presence. He messed up often and totally, but he knew whose heels to follow hard after to help him go forward while tripping over humanity.

Chased by grace. Caught by grace.

Once I believed I could outrun the Father while He relentlessly chased after me on a crooked path. And later, I foolishly believed I was the one who had to do the chasing to catch enough of Him to get it right.

We see how the Father wants to be in His children's lives from the beginning of His story. Sadly, sin created the hiding place where we can be seen. With one hand on a fig leaf and one hand wiping food off their face, the Father's first garden-offspring couldn't stand near Holiness. How can we desire His presence in the same way He desires ours?

And they heard the sound of the Lord God walking in the garden in the cool of the day and the man and his wife hid themselves from His presence among the trees (Genesis 3:8 ESV).

It's surreal that from the beginning of time we have been able to experience the presence of a holy God, and yet we desperately ignore the rustling of the trees.

Sin, the great divide. Jesus, the great bridge. In-dwelt, we don't have to chase what we already possess. We can experience His presence by simply standing on what we have.

Are you chasing or running away?

Voice in the Cornfield

The sheep hear his voice, and he calls his own sheep by name and leads them out. John 10:3

We live in a noisy world.

Consider the never-ending barrage of voices assailing us every day in our homes, at work, and especially from the media. Our head is overfed with social invasion.

It's enough to make me run to a quiet place. Shhh, the silent place powered by mules.

The other day I needed a break from life, agendas, and digital exhaustion. I needed to hear only One voice. My usual sanctuary can be found in the cornfield in Lancaster County.

Where can we go to *be still* and know that He is God? Where can we go to *be*?

Once upon a time in a rural land, while our children were growing up, we lived in a farmhouse hugged by cornfields. They knew just where to find me for the prayer-pauses, when faith was a seed in broken earth. Among the corn.

You should join me in the silence where you can hear a seed drop into fallowed ground and grow tall stalks that block the view of the world. A sacred place of solitude, and I go there desperately to seek the sound of God. I know we're to live by faith and not the audible words resounding in the sheaves, but . . . I hear. *I do.*

However, many times when sound was stilled, I spent times chatting to the sky and often wondered if only the ears of corn were listening. And yet, when He calls me to the closet in the meadow, I go, even in winter when fields are as leveled as I am. It's when I hear life quietly waiting to grow in idle earth.

Jesus withdrew to mountains and gardens when He experienced the same problem—the loudness of multitudes.

Do you have a secret chamber where you hear His voice above it all?

Be still,
AND KNOW THAT
I am
GOD
Psalm 46:10

Shifting Seasons

Let me hear in the morning of your steadfast love for in You I trust. Make me know the way I should go, for to you I lift up my soul. Psalm 143:8 ESV

Most of us look forward to the changing of seasons, especially when earth turns technicolor. I do. But then there's the other side when clocks turn ahead and speed time and darkness. It's all about the focus.

It's the same with our personal seasons—when frailty collides with the way we see the moment. Once again as this season of crisis would have it, I'm spending a few calendar pages in hospitals and nursing facilities among those who begged against it. Every one of them once expected to stay well and able. *I just know it.*

So, I deliberately pause in the corridors to observe once-strong men who provided for families, now depending on chairs with wheels to move them from one place to another. Today my husband is one of them. I look past the fragile to the once-capable women who raised babies and kept homes but now sit alone in an antiseptic room filled with memories held in a picture frame.

They have a story of when time stood still yet passed so quickly. It triggers despair if I look at their *now*—but they had a *then.* Thankfully, we have had a *then.*

To have hope in the no-matter-the-season may sound like fluff-filled answers rather than a sure promise from the One who can spin it into gold. And I've seen it happen—haven't you?

We can count on the fact that nothing stays the same. Life is a surprise of changing seasons. David went from a sheep pasture to a throne. Peter was a fisherman who became the rock of the church. Joseph went from pit to palace to rule Egypt. And teenage Mary went from peasant to parent of the Messiah.

Grace gives the ability to embrace the season.

When God rearranges our lives, our responsibility is to rearrange our focus. We can choose to see the bittersweet-ness of autumn—and ourselves—as a multi-colored glow or the withered and fallen that once was. And when we notice that life is a cache of colored moments of grace, we can see the days ahead from a different view.

What is your view of this season?

Stone Free

What shall I render to the Lord for all his benefits to me? Psalm 116:12 ESV

Some say they don't want to read the Bible because it has stories of wrath, war, and scandal. Yet don't we curiously listen to the media overturn lives repeatedly? Scandal sells.

Yes, Scripture is filled with stories of scandal, because first-century people weren't any different than us. Humans are human.

Think of the story of the redeemed adulteress in the gospel of John (8:1–11). Publicly exposed for her sin by the pious, the frightened woman is dragged by the Pharisees to the temple steps. Barefoot and disheveled, she is thrown into the dark gaze of her enemies but looks up to see One whose eyes look like God's.

The accusers ask Jesus, "The law of Moses says this woman must be stoned to death. What do you say?" The inquiry is a trap to have Him judge the scarlet-letter lady. If He said she could go free, well, you know, then He'd be the law-breaking Messiah.

No debate as Jesus kneels low to scribble. A hush comes over the crowd while the holy finger writes in the dust.

What did He write – Their names- their sins- Ours?

"Anyone who has never sinned, throw the first stone," says the only One who is qualified.

Every eye looks down to the ground where they drop the *stone-unthrown.* They leave one by one, first the older men, then the others.

Jesus kneels low to write once again and asks where the woman's accusers have gone. Compassion and righteousness stands before the broken one who has been made whole, and tells her to go and sin no more.

You and me—we're on both sides of the line in the dust. Like the accusers, we have held a pocketful of stones waiting for someone to get caught in the act. And like her, we have sinned and Jesus was right there to stand up for us.

On a cross.

She expected to be shamed to death. Instead, she was commissioned to live a new life. *Like us.*

When has the Lord stood up for you when others wanted to throw stones?

My Begats

For the Lord is good; His loving kindness is everlasting and His faithfulness to all generations. Psalm 100:5

How many of us know the name of our great-grandmother? Or our great-greats? Unless you've done an ancestry search, I'm guessing you're guessing.

I have a Sara Jane and a plain Sarah. I also have a John Henry Carter way high on the family tree, the only believing relative I'm aware of. Years ago I did a genealogical dig complete with photos and stories. One family member was displeased with me for overturning dirt.

But really, dear aunt, don't you know that most of us come from a mixed heritage? We all have it—even Jesus.

It would be nice to boast of lineage of those coming over on the *Mayflower*, but my family is more like the Irish immigrants stowed in steerage on the *Titanic*. Either way, our family is a treasured heirloom and we get only one group of humans assigned to us by God's creative design and DNA.

Not even Jesus had a sinless line. In the first seventeen verses of the first chapter of the gospel of Matthew, we see a list of boring begats—or are they? Genealogies are important because they demonstrate the mystery and majesty of God's plan.

A few identifiable names among the unpronounceable include four women. In a time when women were not included in Jewish history, only father to son, it's amazing to see the feminine recorded as part of the royals leading up to the birth of the Messiah.

God-inspired Scripture tells of the ancestry scattered with shame. Jesus wanted His family recorded. *All of them.*

Tamar, the scheming widow, yearned for offspring and posed as a shrine prostitute to trick her father-in-law, Judah, resulting in pregnancy to preserve the line (Genesis 38).

Rahab, the Jericho harlot, sheltered spies and later was known for faith and courage (Joshua 2).

Bathsheba, the woman involved in infidelity with King David, years later became the mother of Solomon, an ancestor of Jesus (2 Samuel 11).

And the dear one, Ruth, different from the other ladies, was from the despised nation of Moab. Ruth was not a Jewess, yet God chose her to be in the line of the Kinsman Redeemer (Ruth 1–4).

Worthy accounts of a turn-around . . . a desperate housewife, two prostitutes, and an adulteress, all part of the Messianic family tree.

The stories are not about sin. The stories are about grace.

Our Savior had a background much like you and me. Every one of us has a lifeline stained with sin, which is the glorious reason for verse 18 in Matthew 1, "Now the birth of Jesus was as follows . . ."

When I look through tattered scrapbooks filled with black and white remembrances of long ago, I see grace on every page. To my great-greats, I can leave a blessing or a curse by the way I live.

How can your life influence the next generation?

God's Breath

All Scripture is breathed out by God and profitable for teaching, for reproof, for correction, and for training in righteousness. 2 Timothy 3:16 ESV

The Bible can be a pretty intimidating book. This week I spoke with a young woman who shared how she experiences peace when she reads the Bible but isn't sure how to gain a personal understanding of Scripture. She's not alone.

Shortly after my conversion, I began noticing how I was neglecting God's Word. I read plenty of books about faith but couldn't seem to get past the thee-thou-begats in the Bible. So Christian books seemed an easier read. The Bible seemed to be somewhat irrelevant for my current times as I tore through the ancient Genesis drama to the Gospels. I became bored with chronology, genealogy and cubits.

So, I purchased a child's version of the Bible with the passages in pictures and speech balloons to help me have a better understanding. *Don't laugh.* Not my suggestion to anyone, but it worked for me, and before I knew it I could feel God's breath and hear His heart on every page.

It tells us in 2 Timothy 3:16 that all Scripture, all sixty-six books, is inspired by God. *Inspired* means breathed into (*theopneustos*). His breath is all over the stories of real people in real time, who made real mistakes and met a real God. I'm grateful for human scribes like Moses, David, Paul, and John, who were divinely inspired by a holy Author to write it down.

I had a desire to know what it meant for me. I joined a small women's Bible study that helped develop my love for Scripture, and nearly thirty years ago I found a Precept Inductive Bible study written by Kay Arthur that taught me how to study and understand the sacred depth within the Word of God.

I learned three steps to revelation: observe, interpret, and apply. It goes like this . . . what does the text say, what does it mean, and what does it mean for me? And all these years later, I certainly don't understand it all, but cling to and trust what I *do* understand.

So, if you're like I once was and don't know where to begin, may I encourage you to open your Bible and try these few steps:

Set aside a quiet time.

Choose a place with no distractions, a sanctuary in a corner.

Bring a journal and a pen and listen hard.

Prepare your heart in prayer.

Try this: Use a psalm to praise, Psalm 32 to confess, the gospel of Matthew 6:9–12 to present needs, and Philippians 4:6 to express gratitude. As you dig deep, you will undoubtedly fall deeper in love with Jesus.

What gets in the way of spending time in God's Word? What changes can you make?

Margins and Moments

Do not be conformed to this world, but be transformed by the renewal of your mind, that by testing you may discern what is the will of God, what is good and acceptable and perfect. Romans 12:2 ESV

Are you enjoying life? Honest answer.

Life goes fast—we have very little margin anymore. I had more time years ago meeting the needs and schedules of a husband, four children, and a home, than I do now. It's crazy.

Most of us are living at a pace that's unsustainable and unbiblical. I had a few special moments with close friends the other evening. One of the first things we talked about was stress and overload. We all seem to be on the same wheel and don't know how to get off.

The next morning, I took inventory of priorities and commitments. Hmm, still didn't see the problem. I had to wonder if I was doing a lot of good things or if I was doing the *best* things?

Normal is busy today, but I don't want to be normal. I see people everywhere multitasking, putting eyeliner on at the traffic light or while still driving (yikes!), gulping lunch in the parking lot, abbreviating life to meet the hurried moment, all while having constant electronic interruptions.

I heard somewhere that if the devil can't make us really bad, then he'll make us really busy.

We're so extended, we don't have enough time to engage in meaningful relationships with family and friends anymore. I can remember when Sunday was the day to simply rest and enjoy family. It's not happening.

So what can we do? We can't create time, but we can create moments. So, I challenge us . . .

Start at the beginning. Sunday. Let's think how we can hallow this sacred day. Then, on the other six days, create a to-don't list. In between, find time to talk to a ninety-year-old and ask what they would have done differently, even though their days seemed to have more hours.

I doubt you'll hear them say, "I wish I worked longer hours." But they might say, "I wish I enjoyed more sunsets and ice cream."

Life is speeding by. We have twenty-four hours to catch up and begin creating margins and moments.

What can you do differently tomorrow that stole a piece of today?

The Scent of Remembrance

But thanks be to God, who in Christ always leads us in triumphal procession, and through us spreads the fragrance of the knowledge of Him everywhere.
2 Corinthians 2:14 ESV

What things come to mind when you breathe in a certain scent?

It's amazing how only five senses can connect us to the world around us. Consider just the unique gift of smell that can mystically transport to visions of the past in one momentary whiff. Like unlocking a treasure chest and having a memory come out in a fragrance.

Pause and think of what scent causes you to revisit a special place in your story. I realize some memories can smell like a wet dog, but for this moment think of something that takes you to a sweet place of contentment.

For me, fragrant flashbacks of paste and crayons reopens Miss Zerdans' first grade classroom door at Trevose Elementary School. Smelled like *beginnings.*

And I quickly revisit Gramma's house of mothballs and gardens of boxwood with one nostalgic inhale. The fresh smell of laundry on the line transfers me to the hem of my mother's apron, where I learned to count clothespins.

And then there's the first-date violets. Smelled like *innocence.*

Nothing compared to the sweet scent of my baby's breath and powdered bottom—the incense of new life wrapped swaddling tight for a *lifetime memory.*

And the ones that leave tracks on my heart . . . fresh-picked lilacs pruned close off the branch clutched tight in little hands to deliver to the nursery school teacher—and better yet, the cider simmering on a wood-burning stove always smelled like the kids were coming home from long-ago school days. Smelled like a *piece of my heart.*

After my mom passed away, I attempted to preserve her unforgettable scent by keeping an article of clothing in a zip-lock bag. Over time, it faded. She never wore perfume. She just smelled like *Mom*—more costly than anything bottled.

I even remember the fragrance of the dear lady who prayed me through the veil after I walked down the aisle to Jesus, way back in '75. Smelled like *freedom.*

And then there is the first time I smelled crisp pages in my first Bible. Smelled like *deliverance.*

Some things will lose their scent, but the life-giving fragrance of Christ can never diminish. Smells like *life.*

What scent is your sweet remembrance?

Dressed to Bless

So, as those who have been chosen of God, holy and beloved, put on a heart of compassion, kindness, humility, gentleness and patience. . . . Beyond all these things put on love. Colossians 3:12, 14

Clothing is a funny thing. It's just fabric and thread. As women we sometimes focus more than we need to on our wardrobe. Or do we?

You might be surprised how often the Bible talks about clothing. It begins right there in the beginning. In the garden, while Adam and Eve were having a forbidden bite to eat, they realized they were naked and saw themselves differently. Trying to hide their nakedness, they sewed fig leaves to cover themselves. The Creator had to step in and design something better—animal skins. The wardrobe required blood, symbolic of Jesus who covers us in His sacrifice.

New clothes, a robe of righteousness hanging right there in the gospel of Genesis. In Christ we receive new clothing, but sometimes we insist on tearing through the closet of our lives and bring out the old . . . the comfortable.

The good news is, we can cast off the undesirable garments that no longer fit. Colossians 3:8 tells to "Cast off and throw away all these rotten garments of anger, wrath, malice, slander, and obscene talk from your mouth. (ESV)

Our new wardrobe can be found in Colossians 3:12, 14. Sweet reasonableness. What a great-layered look.

Years ago we attended a wedding where a stunning bride clothed in her ivory-pure *stunned* everyone with her foul reaction to stepping on her hem. It didn't fit the moment and stained the image of her beauty. Have you ever tread on your image of beauty?

What we choose to wear each day is vital to our reflection as the daughter of the King. We have the choice to adorn ourselves in a timeless ensemble that lasts eternally or to meet the frustrating moment of stepping on our hem and reacting poorly.

Just strip and hang up the hang-ups. Try on your new clothes adorned in the jewel of Jesus and see how many say you are *becoming.*

Have you kept some of your "old comfortables" to wear under your new clothes?

Hemline Faith

And when the woman saw that she had not escaped notice, she came trembling and fell down before Him, and declared in the presence of all the people the reason why she had touched Him, and how she had been immediately healed. And He said to her, "Daughter, your faith has made you whole; go in peace." Luke 8:47–48

Are you looking for light in a dark place—or maybe looking for something to hold onto because you feel as though life is slipping straight through your clenched hands.

When I was seven years old, Hurricane Hazel ripped hard through Bucks County. Power outages and blizzard winds uprooted tall trees from the earth to make me realize things don't always stay in their place. Dark became darker while my mother and I waited for my dad to come home from his night shift. I hated that he wasn't near.

We always seem to look for our dad to be the shelter when we don't know where to turn in the darkness. What added to my fear was when my mom and I met the storm face-to-face on the dark path behind the house leading to the cellar fuse box. The strong gusts tried to separate us, and I clutched the edge of her skirt and wouldn't let go. The lantern was torn from her grip, and for a moment she seemed gone as she ran after it. I still remember groping blindly for her fluttering cotton skirt, because . . .

I knew she was as close as her hem.

One of the stories in Scripture that speaks so personally to me is of one of my favorite ladies—the woman who reached out to touch the hem of Jesus' garment as He walked through the crowd. For years she sought help from physicians, but none could make a difference. She thought she went unnoticed among the mass of people pressing in on Jesus. In desperation she reached out to touch the robe's holy edge. He asked who touched Him when He felt His power pour out.

The unnoticed was suddenly noticed when Jesus turned to her and called her "Daughter." On that day, countless people brushed against the Messiah but only one truly touched Him.

Our soul gets crowded and we become heart-sore when marriages bend and finally break, when sickness comes to stay, and jobs shut, finances fail, and wandering children fall off the edge of belief . . . and we feel alone in the dark, looking for the shelter of a Father.

When we feel unnoticed—unanswered—we can do more than brush against Jesus. The power of God is within our reach. He is waiting to speak "Daughter" and wholeness over our lives. We can open our empty hands and cling to the One who leads us through dark places because . . .

He is as close as His hem.

Are you reaching out in the darkness?

Faith

The Beautiful No

I'm guessing you're like me and simply love when God's answer is yes to a fervent prayer. And why wouldn't it be? We're all needy and He's all-powerful. It sounds like it should work out well.

When God says no, it doesn't matter about anyone else's yes. Expect a consequence to be attached.

If the answer doesn't conform to our wishful thinking and demanding moment and we don't instantly receive a custom-made miracle, we become bitter and doubtful, because . . . well, you know, God must not be listening. Or there. Or care.

I've begged my Father for many things that have come my way in a completely opposite form because He had something so much better up His sovereign sleeve. I was as disagreeable as a pouty-finite child who stamps her spoiled foot at the heavens because I just didn't see it until I saw it. *Later.*

All of us seem to struggle with God's will. We pray for the lost to be saved and they perish, we pray for those to live and they die, and we pray to get through the day and we don't.

And I don't understand.

But what I *do* understand is that an un-answer doesn't make God any less God. He never gives stones and snakes when we ask for bread and fish.

"If you then, who are evil, know how to give good gifts to your children, how much more will your Father who is in heaven give good things to those who ask Him!" (Matthew 7:11 ESV).

So, what if we believed God was actually good? And what if we discovered the lesson buried in the rubble of the beautiful no? Our view of life would be changed.

I look back on life when I could see only through my wish-sized view, and He had the bigger picture already hanging on my wall. And I thank Him for not giving me over to foolish requests.

I have journals filled with a mix of miracles and unanswered prayer, and I need to read one page so I can get through to the next.

If our belief is big enough to believe that God is big enough to answer in the right time, in the right way, then we're only one faith-filled prayer away from the miracle.

So, I encourage you, and me, to keep asking, seeking, and knocking, and to be assured that He is on the way to the door.

What is an unanswered prayer you can give thanks for?

What's Love Got to Do with It?

Let us know, let us press on to know the Lord; his going out is sure as the dawn. Hosea 6:3 ESV

The tangled love story of Hosea and Gomer is an unforgettable picture of God's covenant love for His people. We sometimes shy away from the book of Hosea because it can be confusing, but if you want to see Jesus in the Old Testament, it's a must-read.

The real-life couple star in the ancient soap opera about an unusual marriage between the prophet and the prostitute. The story begins with Jehovah God instructing Hosea to find a wife—a harlot.

Sounds absurd, I know, but it has a beautiful purpose. It always does.

So the preacher obeyed and gave the fallen lady his name. They set up housekeeping and started a family. The names of the children weren't anything I'd want embroidered on my baby's layette: *God Scatters, No Mercy,* and *Not My People.* Before long, Gomer lived up to her tainted reputation and continued a love affair with the world. Despite Hosea's patient pleas, her bitter betrayal took her far from home and she refused to return. He adored her, but still she abandoned him.

A broken vow . . . a broken heart . . . a broken life. Sounds familiar.

When we turn our back on God, He doesn't wait for us to come back. He pursues us. Hosea's beautiful words still talk to the church today about our unfaithfulness and His extravagant forgiveness.

Later, the Lord spoke to him again and told him to take back the wife he couldn't stop loving. He found her battered by life, chained in a slave auction. The broken-hearted one purchased her for silver and barley.

He paid a price for his bride. Sounds familiar.

This story of redemption portrays God's beautiful desire to make us His own. No matter how unfaithful you and I have been, we can find redeeming arms to hold us close.

If you want to read a good love story, just pick up your Bible. Only fourteen chapters tell about their love story. And ours.

How has God been faithful to you even when you have been unfaithful to Him?

Empty Nest Season

There is an appointed time for everything.
Ecclesiastes 3:1

It's September, and children of all ages and stages seem to be going somewhere. And then . . .

The bittersweet-ness of autumn when in a blink a full house becomes an empty nest. Home-sweet-nest changes in a nanosecond, and somehow the fridge is full, the house stays clean, and the hum of the washer is resting. Your schedule that once belonged to them, is now yours. How did something that took so long happen so quickly?

Teething, bad dreams, and skinned knees are all part of being a mom who mends. Like Father, who mends the mom's skinned heart when babies leave for kindergarten, college, and finally (deep breath) have grown and flown.

What mom can't relate?

I remember yesterday-today, when my children took steps into the world without me.

I cried like they died. I'd visit the museum of their room and smell the sweet scent of where they'd lain their head. When I could say goodnight and love them to the moon.

When our youngest child left the nest, my husband stood on the porch until baby son's taillights disappeared into the night. He kept watch and said goodnight under his breath.

What dad can't relate?

Blink. Blink.

And now daughter has her own emptying nest to cope with. Her son marries and moves to another state, quickly followed by the missionary daughter who goes off to another country. But one left—sometimes.

What gramma can't relate?

We've prepared them to leave home, but somehow we haven't prepared ourselves. As parents, we get a little over two decades to get ready. But we're never ready.

Seasons change. Now what do we do beyond the momma years when we're forced to retire? We don't. We retire on our knees, always praying for the one under the new roof.

If you are a pre-nester and still have teenagers at home, hug the moment. If you are a post-nester, enjoy *you* and take silent steps to press deeper into the Father, the One who mends the bruised heart of the mom (and dad) of the fledging.

Breathe in and whisper out . . . this is simply a transition and a fresh season. And tell yourself that *you've done well.*

Think of a bittersweet transition that ultimately resulted in blessing.

Do You Want to Get Well?

And at once the man was healed, and he took up his bed and walked. John 5:9 ESV

It's feast time in the city. The Lamb enters through the Sheep Gate into Jerusalem and chose to walk among the lame, blind, and withered. (Over the course of my young life, I was all three waiting for someone to come along and change my situation.)

Jesus stops to ask a wild question: "Do you ever want things to be different?" (my paraphrase).

In John 5:1–9, we see one who stayed sick until He met Jesus. There he was, lying next to healing waters and yet he remained paralyzed for thirty-eight years. This man was like the many infirm that lined the floors waiting for an annual angel visit to come and stir the Bethesda miracle-mercy pool. Waiting for the waters to move because their limbs couldn't.

As I read this gospel story, I can smell the sickness while walking past the emaciated, and I can see the haunting glances and vacant faces pleading for healing mercy. Can you?

It's not just a biblical scene from thousands of years ago in a holy city; it's a scene from today, every day . . . when we pass by the hurting and withered in spirit in the workplace, in the grocery line, in the news. *In the pews.*

Jesus had a holy knack of asking the most pointed questions. You could ponder for a lifetime before you discover yourself enough to answer honestly.

So, Jesus looks into the face of one (and all) and asks, "Do you want to get well?" And the afflicted feebly looks up and says, "I can't. I need someone to help."

What if the paralytic responded with a "No, thanks, I'm fine. I can just hang here for the next other half of my life and keep waiting for someone to throw me into the healing place I need to go."?

Sometimes afflictions can define us if we let them.

The merciful Healer doesn't pick him up and toss him in. Instead, He speaks life: "Rise and walk."

Many of us truly cannot physically get up, but we can spiritually *rise* up above our excuses, emotional wounds, and unhealthy patterns that keep us paralyzed on the ground. We have to get up from the place of *no, thanks.*

Sometimes it's easier to stay the way we are. The real question tucked inside this one is, "Do you want to be changed?" But then, well, you know, we might have to *change* and quit blaming others for our condition.

Jesus was forcing the invalid to realize that as long as he blamed others for his problem, he'd never get better.

If we truly wish to get well, we must look to the One who stirs us to wholeness. He is waiting for the answer to His wild question.

Everybody into the pool!

Just answer this: Do you want to get well?

Where is Your Faith?

And he said to them, "Where is your faith?" Luke 8:25

Here's another one of those questions that Jesus asks that makes us think—don't you think? And He knows just when to ask. Jesus asked the disciples, "Where is your faith?" in the middle of a storm. He's been asking me the same in the middle of mine.

So, I place myself right back there in the raging storm, inside the wind-battered, water-filled boat of Luke 8:22–25, and it's easy to wonder if my faith fell out onto the sleeping Jesus and got swallowed up in the dark waves.

Be there for a moment and locate your faith.

My answer to His divine inquiry might be, "My faith is on the shoreline where it's safe."

And so they cry out, "Lord, we're perishing." It was enough to make the Master awaken and rebuke the danger. He does the same for us today when we feel desperate.

This is what I love about the story. Jesus said to His disciples, "Let *us* go over to the other side of the lake." So *they* got into the boat and set out. The assurance is that Jesus didn't tell them to go it alone.

And isn't it amazing—these men had a disciple-eye's view of Jesus performing miracles of healing and casting demons into pigs and were still afraid of drowning while He was right there!

May I never judge a disciple. I've been in the same boat!

All of us will be touched by events we have no control over, no matter how hard or far we try to row to the other side.

When we're experiencing life's storms and our peace is about to capsize, we must know God's Word for more than a memory verse. We need to believe it belongs to us. Only then can it infuse a strong faith into our pacing soul where worry and despair cannot survive the elements.

Only if we know the Word.

In times when faith and fear come to a swift collision, we need to rehearse the miracles so we don't drown in the circumstances. My journals throw me a lifeline—the keeping place of amazing happenings to remind me of His presence in the whirlwind.

When logic screams, “How?” God whispers, “Remember!” I write this to encourage another’s heart—and my own.

“Faith isn’t a sense, nor sight, nor reason, but simply taking God at His Word.” (Christmas Evans)

Have you experienced a time when sense, sight, or reason got in the way of simply taking God at His Word?

Warfare Garments

Put on the full armor of God, so that you may be able to stand firm against the schemes of the devil. Ephesians 6:11

If you're listening to the news lately, you will agree life is a war zone. In a hurting world of headlines, you may have noticed the lights going down in an already dark world.

We need more than ourselves to get through daily living. We need something so much bigger than us. We need God.

We need Him because we have an enemy who sends fiery deadly D-darts our way: discouragement, doubt, despair, defeat, and, ultimately, destruction.

Unfortunately, it's not a video game where you get to level three by annihilating generated demons that get in the way. There is a reality-realm where we need the unseen clothes to battle the unseen war. Flesh and blood we may be able to handle, but principalities call for supernatural garments.

Think it sounds a little far-fetched? If demons weren't real, Jesus wouldn't have had to cast so many out.

As Christian women, our heart's battle is for our home, marriages, and children in the day of relentless evil. We have weapons of warfare, so we don't have to experience impotence when praying prodigals to return, marriages to be restored, or the needed strength to move our sick bodies. We can be more victorious than ancient warriors.

This day, don't let the enemy of your soul catch you half-dressed. He works around the clock and never calls a truce. So, the next time someone sees you *still standing* and comments on your royal wardrobe, just say, "This old thing—my helmet of salvation? I've had it for years. It still fits!"

Our timeless ensemble, totally vintage, doesn't go out of style.

Paul tells us in Ephesians 6 how to dress for success in six easy steps: stand firm and gird your loins with the belt of truth, put on the breastplate of righteousness, shod feet with the preparation of the gospel of peace, take up the shield of faith to extinguish the flaming missiles, and take the helmet of salvation and sword of the Spirit . . . and don't forget the military order to pray at all times. It keeps everything on!

If you're wondering what shoes to wear to match your outfit—choose the sandals of peace and spread Jesus with every step. Gird up with more than Spanx; make truth your foundation garment!

So—left-hand shield, right-hand sword . . . boots on the ground. Are you ready to face the day?

When We're Honest

Do your best to present yourself to God as one approved, a worker who has no need to be ashamed, rightly handling the Word of truth. 2 Timothy 2:15 ESV

If you reside on earth, with people, you've been lied to or lied about. And it hurts. And I expect, you have lied to or lied about someone. And it hurts. Every one of us has been broken by someone bending the truth.

Unfortunately, we don't have to be taught how to lie. It begins when we learn how to talk. Honestly, when is the last time you tweaked the truth?

For me, it was as recently when someone asked how I was. Auto-response says, "Oh, I'm fine." Or, it was when someone offended me (yes, there's that word) and I answered with a little white, "That's okay. I'll get over it."

It could have been something bigger when I compromised and said something was right that wasn't. And so, I hate when I lie to myself . . .

I remember as a child having my mouth washed out with soap, horrible-tasting green Palmolive to be exact. Dove would've probably been less repulsive and somewhat more spiritual. Today, I could declare abuse and my poor mom, who simply wanted an honest kid, would be hauled off to jail.

Scripture tells us that God hates a liar. It's what got us into this mess. Lies are as old as the devil. Especially the one that says he is just a medieval fairy tale. Crafty.

What else could've tripped up the sandals of the mighty ones who walked before us, like Abraham, Sarah, Jacob, Rachel, David, and Peter? They all fell into a place where they had to lie their failing-human way out.

Just like them—just like us.

We can learn from their flaws and our own that distances us from the God of truth. If we rehearse a lie enough times, it can re-create our reality and become our story. Think about it.

In the fragile culture of today, we wear a mask and live life hidden, afraid to say who we are, who God is—and that Christ's salvation is the only way out. You may have noticed, it has even become harder to find the truth in churches.

And why is it important to live authentically? Because bending truth breaks. It divides marriages, families, and friends.

What would happen if we became pathologically honest? Try it for a day. It's deeper than *break a habit, make a habit.* Instead of covering up the truth of who we are and what we believe, we can cover ourselves in an Ephesians wardrobe nicely accessorized with the belt of truth. It always holds up our righteousness!

Think about today. Just today. Have you been truthful with others, yourself . . . God?

Wounds and Wonders

And you shall remember the whole way that the Lord you God has led you these forty years in the wilderness, that he might humble you, testing you to know what was in your heart, whether you would keep his commandments. Deuteronomy 8:2 ESV

It was a September Sunday in the year 1975, when four words changed the course of life. And that was exactly 14,914 days ago and all the in-betweens that came from a moment when *just as I am* reluctantly went to a church service by way of a child's hand. And so, a wretch like me had a plan of escape, so I hid out of view in the back pew near the closest exit.

Try to make sense out of mysterious ways. As far away as I was from God, that's how near He was to me. Because for some *unknown* reason, it all came about because I enrolled my kids in a Christian school affiliated with a church that had the handy out-of-view-pew waiting just for the likes of me.

And yes, I remember the exact day and divine instant when Mercy met me in the middle of my madness. The historic marker in life remains a monument.

However, I don't remember one word the pastor said that morning, other than four: "Come as you are." I was sure he must have been talking to those who deserved to be in the front-row seat, but before I knew what happened, I was on my way down the aisle and took a fortunate fall at the feet of Jesus.

I walked out of there not knowing any more than when I walked in, except that life stopped and started. Over.

And it began with one step in a different direction.

So, the story changed—and I love to tell the story. Sharing our faith story isn't about trying to change the way others think; it's about changing the way they hope.

And we all need hope . . .

My testimony, and yours, is precious gold woven through each holy moment of wounds and wonders along our path. It can be the jewel you offer to someone that will bring hope.

We're all in a different place—some starting a journey, some tired from the journey, and some who don't know where they are on the journey. Each milestone charts grace along the way, and mercy will collide right in the place where you're fainting.

The Israelites had pillars and manna to keep them on course for a forty-year trek to remind them of God's faithfulness. I've had amazing experiences for the same four-decade time to prove the power and mercy of a real and on-time God.

Tell your story of God's faithfulness and make someone's day. They're dying to hear it. What has God done in your life to tell His story?

There Comes a Time

You crown the year with Your goodness and Your paths drip with abundance. Psalm 65:11 NKJV

What new beginning do you need? I ask myself that question every new year. There comes a time when we all need a new start. A time when we say I can't do this any longer, I must have something change. And we want to do something to bring it about. But we're limited. If we weren't, we wouldn't make so many temporary resolutions at the turn of a new year and fail miserably before the first day ends.

I'd rather look to a solution than a resolution.

So often at the beginning of the year, I look to a name of God within a special word to hold onto for the next dozen months. This year the word *peace* came to heart. I wondered how, this year especially? My husband suffering, medical bills piling high, and days filled with everything but peace.

However, a few weeks after Christmas, on the heels of celebrating the birth of the Prince of Peace, I was reminded there is no greater shelter than the peace and presence of our Jehovah Shalom.

So, when you think of the coming months, what do you hope will be different? I have several answers, but I'll share the first that comes to mind—me. I want *me* different . . . to genuinely experience the peace that passes understanding in the midst of grieving.

While re-reading the arduous journey logged in last year's journal, I note between the bitter lines and desperately highlight the grace. And when circumstances don't appear to change and we're waiting for something different, can we do that? Highlight the grace, I mean.

The bag we drag may be so heavy we can't take another step to safely walk onto the page of January 1st. Life situations and marred memories can't mysteriously be torn away with the turn of a calendar page—oh, but they can—if we choose to see them differently in perfect abandon.

True peace isn't the absence of problems, it's holding tight to the One who knows how to manage the mess and clean up the spills of our failures. For me, and maybe for you, there's a lot that closes this year that will still be there tomorrow. And, so will He.

So I'm laying down my heavy bag and packing light with just a 2016 survival kit—a Bible filled with miracles and mercy and a new journal to record them. All of them.

I wrote this piece on the eve of a new year, never dreaming of the different and uncertain beginning that was about to touch my broken life. Widowhood.

It doesn't need to be a new year, just simply a new day, and may we lean hard close to the Lord of new beginnings and hear Him whisper, "Let's start over," even when we hesitate to believe that we are able.

What is your start-over? Can you trust God enough to follow a new and unknown path?

The Fragrance of Broken

And he said to the woman, "Your faith has saved you; go in peace." Luke 7:50 ESV

Imagine the scene . . . a fine dinner fit for a Pharisee, yet an immoral woman crashed the party. A woman of the city.

Dusty roads brought Jesus to the house of Simon. Custom and hospitality would have the host wash a guest's travel-worn feet with water and anoint their head with oil. Ignored guest Jesus reclines at the table when a fallen woman enters to fall right in His dust.

The intruder came prepared to anoint and worship. So, come and sit at the table she kneels beneath. Grateful, humble, and with trembling boldness, she pours her best over Him and wipes His feet with tears and a costly perfume from an alabaster box. Locks of love, unveiled, wipe up the beauty. She "wastes" her best on Him, says one. And yet the Forgiver pours His best on her, and on us, from the cross.

She cleanses His feet. He cleanses her heart. Then she is welcome at the table, no longer on the floor.

The extravagant worship-woman recorded in Luke 7:36–50 tells the same truth but a different account recorded in the other three gospels. The lady went outside of culture and custom to worship the One who loved her first. When she bowed humble-low and looked up into His eyes, He looked into her soul, knowing her better than anyone, better than any accuser or judge.

The unnamed woman of scandalous grace entered bound by the past and left set free with the fragrance of wholeness.

Jesus uses broken vessels. His sweet holy scent is released through the cracks and the breaks. Do you carry the fragrance of being in His presence?

Six Impossibles Before Breakfast

Alice laughed. "There's no use trying," she said: "one *can't* believe impossible things."

"I daresay you haven't had much practice," said the Queen. "When I was your age, I always did it for half-an-hour a day. Why, sometimes I've believed as many as six impossible things before breakfast."[1]

Do you remember eavesdropping in Wonderland as a child, overhearing the exchange between Alice and the Queen? I'm with the Queen. Unlike Alice, I've had much practice believing "the impossibles" in our family. Curiouser and curiouser is the amazing power of Jehovah God.

Trying to understand things that seem unattainable make Him very small . . . like us. Go ask Alice, when she's ten feet tall. We can be larger than our circumstances.

While reading in the gospel of John this morning, I believed six—no, seven, really—impossible things before breakfast. The miraculous works of Jesus when turning water

---

[1] Lewis Carroll, *Through the Looking Glass* (Philadelphia: Henry Altemus Company, 1897), 102.

into fine wine, healings and cures, exorcisms, leaving footprints on water, feeding the masses with the catch of the day, and oh . . . raising the dead. All sound impossible, but very possible with the supernatural God who is not about fiction.

Believe is woven through the gospel of John ninety-nine times. The word (*pisteuo*) means confident trust and persuasion.

I trust because I am persuaded.

Our God masters in things that can't be done. When we find it difficult to believe truths that tease our reason, lean into the deep six: John 3:16; 2 Timothy 2:13; Hebrews 13:5; 1 John 1:9; Psalm 46:1; and John 14:3.

What is your impossible situation? What does God's Word say you can believe?

Web of Control

There was a time when I thought I was in control of nearly everything. Rule by the toxic-two, perfectionism and guilt, was absolutely debilitating. It didn't make it easier that I wasn't good at delegating. I thought I could do it faster and better.

Come now, you know I'm not alone.

I tired myself out trying to be the perfect wife and mother, the organic super-homemaker who baked whole grain breads, ironed on Monday, scrubbed floor corners with a toothbrush, polished my plant dirt, twice on holidays . . .

The kids had to be shiny and perfect. What a web and chain. For them, and for me.

Oh, but it got worse. I was sure my inner control freak could fix broken people. Life happened and spun out of control, and I realized I was the most broken of all.

It must be God's universe and not mine.

The story of Peter (he has his own book, you know) helped me see that God chooses the imperfect. The foot-in-the-mouth, fallible-fisher-of-men, follower-denier was chosen the head honcho of the inner circle twelve. The rock God built His church upon.

I love how the Bible tells the truth about frail humans.

I have a close author-friend who can relate to me, and you, and Peter. Lady Lori, self-made sweat-and-success story, hit some bumps and pulled herself up by her pink-pump straps every time. Until.

The Blessed-Controller of all things had the super-gal remove her shoes to stand on holy ground in abandonment to His greatness.

I love her story—it tells mine. And maybe yours?

I pray that the eyes of your heart may be enlightened so that you may know what is the hope of His calling, what are the riches of the glory of His inheritance in the saints, and what is the surpassing greatness of His power toward us who believe. These are in accordance with the working of the strength of His might.
Ephesians1:18–19

We can become perfectly imperfect by letting go. What is holding onto you that you have trouble giving to God's capable control?

Beyond the Veil

This hope we have as an anchor of the soul, a hope both sure and steadfast and one which enters within the veil. Hebrews 6:19

Imagine life without a prayer—for the mother whose son is addicted to drugs, for the man who sits at the bedside of the terminally ill wife, for the abused and confused child. Imagine.

We don't have to imagine life without a prayer—unless we don't pray.

How many people have you spoken with recently who are experiencing a desperate time in need of prayer? I can name several. Almost everyone I come in contact with has something. If they don't ask for prayer, somehow our automatic response is that we say we'll pray. And so, don't you agree there is a need for the power and presence of something far greater than . . . all of this?

But how can the presence of God come to us unless we seek His presence? It's not like He's a distant deity that can't be located.

In the Old Testament, people couldn't just walk into the Holy Place and ask for God's mercy. Mankind was separated from Yahweh with a thread barrier woven strong with sin. The temple veil was sixty feet high, thirty feet wide, and four inches thick.

And man could not move it.

But with the last breath of Jesus, it tore wide open from top to bottom, giving instant access to the holiest place. When He nailed our flawed performance to the cross in the Good Friday moment, it was finished and we are no longer in the outer court.

So instead, imagine that *we* have been given the unique-amazing-too-much-to-comprehend privilege to actually come into the presence of an Almighty God. And be heard.

Now, believe it.

What keeps us from the sacred opportunity? If we're not careful, our neglect will mend the veil and cover our access.

Our mind-set fulfills the "weakly" obligation as pew potatoes by stringing a few stale words to sit before a King. How often I have failed to simply invest time at His feet by allowing things to get in the way.

So, what if you and I clean out a hallowed place in our prayer closet and make room for the throne? Sounds strange, but understand, many times my throne room has been my car or a hospital waiting room, as it is today . . .

Even in the secular or scary, we can still be aware of His glory and tremble in awesome knowledge that we can confidently approach Him. Anywhere, any time, we can experience His faithfulness to show up in the temple of our heart.

And so, we don't have to imagine life without prayer—unless we don't pray. Pray with your pen and scribe for the King.

Stress and Grace

"Therefore do not be anxious for tomorrow; for tomorrow will care for itself. Each day has enough trouble of its own." Matthew 6:34

Are you concerned about tomorrow? You must be.

Stress surrounds us and it seems we react to it far worse than we used to. People are agitated, defensive, and angry. Media voices feed our head and pummel our peace with negative hard drive—and we're wired.

We take pills to start the day . . . we take pills to end the day. Addictions camouflage our reality and anesthetize our cluttered minds. We're sick because we're stressed and stressed because we're sick. Our bodies answer our actions with anxiety, depression, and dependency. Antidepressants are the most frequently prescribed medication of the day, surpassing the second runner-up, high blood pressure management.

And yet we don't seem to get that the only control we have over strain and tension is our response to it.

We live in a modern-day Babylon overwhelmed with desire to live for stuff. We create our own stress with work and financial overload and a rush to keep up with the race of it all. And we long for the days that used to be twenty-four hours.

Rewinding to yesteryear when I was a child, my hard-working dad made time for a nap in a hammock under the shade tree. Rewinding back not quite as far, raising my own children, there was always precious moments for long walks, clothesline chats, and even quilting.

All this didn't just happen. After all, everyone has always had responsibilities to carry out while the hands on a clock spun around, so why does it seem so difficult to make it work now?

And think about how the ancients were plenty stressed and pressed, and could have required therapy and a pill. Abraham faced a mountain and a sacrifice. Moses faced a desert and a sea that needed to open. Noah faced a flood. Joseph faced a pit. Daniel faced a den. David faced a giant. Paul faced a shipwrecked life. And Jesus faced a cross.

So no matter what decade or era, we don't *have* a choice whether we will face the pressure of residing on earth. But, thankfully, we can *make* a choice to either rehearse and react to the tension of life or *"cast all your anxiety on Him because He cares for you"* (1 Peter 5:7 ESV

We can lay our turmoil down upon the grace that is sufficient for each day. You may believe the times we live in are bigger than grace—but nothing is larger than sovereignty.

We can't change what is happening in our world, but we can change our mind-set. Would you believe that the greatest miracle God can do is not in your circumstances—it's in your mind.

Life Saving Verse

Comfortable can be a self-dug pit. That was my residence for quite a while in my young life. Then, something amazing, an altar call a world ago and "just as I am" became "just as I wasn't."

Although my children were tucked away in a back pew at the time, they had a front-row seat of what Jesus can do in someone's life. And it is still difficult to explain how a transformation can happen in the span of a church service that took thirty years to take place. You would've had to be there, and maybe you were, or maybe you are right now.

A short time after my conversion, a dear lady who must've sensed I was a spiritual rookie took me under her wing and told me a few things. She explained the importance of a "life-verse," and for a long time I didn't get it, until I got it.

Out of 31,000 verses in Scripture, one became neon and a luminary to shed light into the dark moment: "I would have despaired if I had not believed I would see the goodness of the LORD in the land of the living" (Psalm 27:13).

There are times the only thing we see is what is in front of us. That's the time we need to look up and not around or we may just notice giants.

So, this is etched in the margin of my Bible, along with fingerprints and tears smearing the memorized:

Life is hard but God is good. If not for the hope that He would come through in this life, I would give up. Victory is not just in heaven but also here on planet earth. No matter how dark the night we should never give up our confidence in God's faithfulness even when feeling like collapsing under the affliction.

Psalm 27 goes on to say in verse 14, "Wait for the LORD; be strong and . . . take courage." I have been a lady-in-waiting for many things, for many years. God-breathed words written on ancient parchment is the one thing that has kept me from despairing. When I'm tangled tight and have questions, I let my verse speak loudly above the sound of life.

What special word has God spoken over your life to have you believe to see His goodness in the land of the living?

What's in a Name?

Those who know Your name will put their trust in You.
Psalm 9:10 ESV

Have you ever looked up the meaning of your name? Did it define you?

I hated my name when I was in school. The only one with the name "Verna" dressed in auburn hair and a bone-skinny frame. Try not to stand out! As I got older, I grew into my name and was grateful to be someone who didn't seem to need a last one.

Besides, it means spring-green, *vernal equinox*. I was born in the spring, and the meaning makes me feel a little hopeful—new beginnings.

Names are of value because they're attached to people. When we get introduced, one of the first things we want to know about someone is their name. *Otherwise, they may just remain an acquaintance.*

In biblical times, names were important because they expressed the character of the person. Names were sometimes symbols of how God changed the lives of people, in the example of Abram to Abraham.

The Hebrew names of God demonstrate His attributes. Years ago I studied a book by Kay Arthur, *Lord, I Want to Know You.* It was then that I discovered the powerful meaning revealed in each name that held the answer to every situation in life.

The very first time we're introduced to God in the pages of the Bible (Genesis 1), we find He is the creator of all things. ***Elohim.*** And we are His personal handiwork.

El Elyon, God Most High, is the sovereign controller of the universe. He sustains us through every stormy trial on earth and is the ruler in heaven (Genesis 14).

El Roi, the God who sees, watches over His creation with His holy eye and knows us by name. We need to remind ourselves of this daily (Genesis 16).

El Shaddai, reveals His bounty as the nourisher and the almighty (Genesis 17).

Adonai, our Master and Owner of it all, is revealed in Genesis 15.

Jehovah Jirah is our provision in want and in plenty (Genesis 22).

Jehovah Rapha, our healer, is the only One who can cure a sin-sick world (Exodus 15).

Jehovah Nissi, our banner, is the One who fights our battles (Exodus 17).

Jehovah Shalom, the God of our peace, is told of in the story of Gideon (Judges 6:22).

Jehovah Sabaoth, the Lord of Hosts, is the army commander to call upon when we sense defeat or lack of strength (1 Samuel 1).

Jehovah Raah is our Shepherd who directs our path and sometimes carries us along the way (Ezekiel 34).

Jehovah Shammah is the Lord who is there. His personal presence surrounds us when we feel abandoned or alone (Ezekiel 48:35).

Scripture commands us to hallow the name of God. The Greek word means to make holy, opposite of common. There is nothing common about the power of peace, provision, healing, and strength provided within every title that can carry us through 24/7/365 from the beginning to the end of our years.

Remember, the first thing we want to know of someone is their name; *otherwise they may remain just an acquaintance.*

Those who know God's name put their trust in Him.

God's name is like His signature securing a promise. What name of God do you need to call upon today?

Believing is Seeing

We've heard seeing is believing, but what if we can't see it? Well then, we need to believe. The Bible says faith is the evidence of things not seen.

This past week I've spoken to a few who feel they are in hopeless situations and need to see past their moment.

Now faith is the assurance of things hoped for, the conviction of things not seen. Hebrews 11:1

How about when faith actually can be defined as *not* believing something in spite of evidence. The diagnosis of no hope, the marriage broken beyond repair, the prodigal too far away . . . the 3-D circumstances that block our view of a life-changing God. It's then we must learn to see what we can't.

Faith is like stepping onto an invisible bridge and knowing it will get us to the other side of our story.

I keep in mind the things the Lord allowed me to see before I saw it. *The things man calls impossible but God doesn't agree.*

So where does faith come from? *Faith comes from hearing and hearing comes from the Word of God (Romans 10:17).*

In the eleventh chapter of Hebrews, we read of the faith-greats and how old wombs were opened and lions' mouths were closed. Walls fell down and seas parted. *The things man calls impossible but God doesn't agree.*

Years ago I had no faith when God unexpectedly interrupted my world with His kingdom. My "me of little faith" became stronger and more perfected through time, trouble, and truth. And faith was fostered in "the waiting room" of unexplainable circumstances.

Why does man reason? Maybe because we think we're smart enough to figure it out. And so, I wonder if God giggles?

Faith defies logic.

We can't explain a sovereign God. If we could, He'd be no bigger than our brain.

I see the prophets' words coming true in current events. Reading the Bible is like reading today's newspaper. So seeing *is* believing.

"Faith is believing in things when common sense tells you not to." (George Seaton)

Is common sense blocking the view?

Believe

Clear as Mud

And he said, "Lord, I believe." And he worshiped Him. John 9:38

Some things we will never understand. When we hear of something that doesn't compute with our thinking, we often find it safer to write it off as soon as logic kicks in.

Certain things can't be explained because they're simply supernatural.

The story of the blind beggar in the gospel of John (9:1–41) tells of the outcast sitting by the roadside. The sound of footsteps pause in front of him, and he thinks someone is there to help him. Instead he overhears, "Who sinned, this man or his parents, that he should be blind?"

He hears a holy voice answer, "It was neither this man or his parents. This happened so the work of God might be displayed in his life." As Jesus spoke, He spit on the ground and made clay to anoint the unseeing eyes. He told the man to go wash in the pool of Siloam, and for the first time, the one without sight sees his reflection in the water and then looks up to see the pure face of God.

Jehovah Rapha uses an RX that seems odd to bring light in the darkness, but His work begins in darkness. It did for me when I was a blind beggar.

And so you see, we can't fathom sovereignty. It's as clear as mud to humans.

This is more than a miracle of healing. It's a story of faith and obedience. Spit-and-mud faith. He can use what appears offensive to give life and sight.

I don't understand why Jesus didn't heal with the power of a word or touch, so I've learned to cling to what I do understand. Jesus saw a stricken soul who wanted to see and He met him in his circumstances. The man had a responsibility with the healing offered to him. We have the choice after receiving sight to get up and see or to stay blind.

We're all born blind. Only God can open our eyes, but we need to be willing to wash the mud from our view and get up and walk out the healing.

I've personally learned much from affliction, light and harsh.

Now close your eyes . . . and now open.

Do you remember when God first opened your eyes?

The Best Offense

Good sense makes one slow to anger, and it is his glory to overlook an offense. Proverbs 19:11 ESV

My mom used to say, "Don't let people get the best of you." Well, I certainly have met people along the way who have tried to drain my best—multiple people, multiple times.

We live in a day when everyone is offended by something. We seem to wake up with an attitude just waiting in our thin-skin to get offended. And, you may have noticed, humans aren't natural forgivers.

Why are we always so easily offended? Or defensive?

Since we're only responsible for us, we need to know how to personally cope in a biblical way. The Bible admonishes us not to be oversensitive, and yet countless times my silent prayer has been, "Lord, may I not take offense" while someone is still speaking in a snarky mode. We're fragile.

I can recall when I thought every little offense was worthy of confrontation. At the time, I believed I had only two choices—do battle or cry, and I *knew* I wasn't going to cry.

Gratefully, I experienced grace.

Some offenses are hard to overlook. I know—*I know!* But it's not worth the alternative of lugging around the weight of bitterness, anger, and lost relationships. When others hurt you, remember your spiritual maturity is on display.

Solomon, the wisest of men says right there in Ecclesiastes, "Do not take to heart all the things that people say, lest you hear your servant cursing you. Your heart knows that many times you yourself have cursed others" (7:21-22 ESV).

So the next time we're tempted to spar, let's ask our offended selves three questions:

Do I need to make a point at the risk of losing a relationship?

Am I right?

No, really. Am I?

If I shift position and stand in the other girl's flip-flops, would I feel the same way? Yep, I understand. Sometimes there's not enough o's in "it's just so-o-o hard." But then we should quickly forgive (since there's not enough a's in graaace) by calling upon our Father to give us the power to do what we are unable to do in our own strength.

Is there an offense you need to overlook?

Who Do You Think You Are?

Some years ago, my granddaughter Brianna and I were getting ready to go for a walk in the cornfield. After I zipped my jacket, the quick-minded seven-year-old looked up and said, "Just look at yourself!"

So I went to look in the mirror and didn't see anything wrong. I looked again and saw everything wrong. I was wearing someone else's jacket. Seriously.

Sometimes we need to just look at ourselves . . . a second time. If we're not careful, we might believe we are more than we are—or less than we were created to be. It's a tricky mix.

Fear of insignificance breeds the result it dreads, and we arrive at the destination we were trying to avoid. Where we live, what we do, what we've done, or negative words spoken over us do not define us. *They can't.*

I've had a few conversations just this past week with people I know well but I actually don't. Me included. It's easy to forget who we are when the world paints over our created image and . . . well, we're tempted to re-shape ourselves.

If we're not careful, sophisticated opinions of today may bend ours, and suddenly our radiance will become dim as we're swept away into the loud crowd.

And so I wonder . . . what are we clothed in when we just take a quick look at ourselves? Are we wearing something that doesn't belong to us?

We won't see our true image in a mirror with eyes wide open. We need to look beyond a broken mirror that magnifies the cracks to see our true identity. The One who creates masterpieces out of shards sees a reflection of radiance— clothed in Him. We can see who we are more clearly when we close our eyes and look through His.

Allow the Father to remind you who you are.

Really are.

Psalm 45:11; Psalm 139:14; Isaiah 64:8

Thanks but No Thanks

In everything give thanks; for this is God's will for you in Christ Jesus. 1 Thessalonians 5:18

Giving thanks when it makes no sense makes no sense. Actually, it does. Scripture tells us to give thanks in every circumstance, even in the rough and raw places that get scarred by too much life.

I asked a wounded friend what she's thankful for. And so, she says the usual "husband, kids, roof over my head." But what if the husband leaves, the kids wander, and the roof caves in—what then?

And what if God stays right where He's always been—right there in the sovereign spot where He has control over it all? Well, there's the gratitude.

We can't change the world—we can only be contented in our own. It's oh-so-easy to get swept into the current culture and lose sight of the meaning of Thanksgiving. Lest we forget our rich history and heritage, the true meaning is to gather and remember the goodness of God.

But often, instead of giving thanks for what we have, we're busy waiting at the retailer's door to find something or *anything* we still need. And before the pumpkin pie is digested and the table cleared, we're lining up for a Black Friday *greeding* frenzy.

Somehow our traditional holiday has been hijacked by relentless commercialism and busyness. It doesn't seem so long ago when the children were sitting around our overcrowded table in our farmhouse taking turns reciting, "I'm thankful for . . ."

Home and hearth, cider warming on an old woodstove added to the charm of their responses and sounded somewhat like a Waltons rerun, but I'm still *so* there . . .

Time passed and most of those who were at the table have also and are no longer occupying a chair. And I miss them. And so I learned to cherish the moment and exchange perfect for *good enough* when I'm tempted to let preparation get in the way.

I used to be a Martha. In the familiar story of Mary and Martha (Luke 10), we learn how to find the importance of being rather than doing. Martha is busy being busy and Mary is being still.

And isn't it hard to do, with all the to-do?

Overdrive and stress collides with choosing the necessary—the sacred place—and we settle for crumbs and expect the Lord to, as well.

And there's no room for thanks at Thanksgiving.

Martha chose preparation over visiting, and Mary chose spending time with Jesus over preparation. I'm thinking there's a little of both in each of us. So, may we redirect our fussing to focusing on the good portion as we serve our families well, like Martha . . . and serve our Master well, like Mary.

Then we'll be able to say together, "First I'm thankful that I'm thankful."

What are you most thankful for?

First Love

I know you are enduring patiently and bearing up for my name's sake, and you have not grown weary. But I have this against you, that you have abandoned the love you had at first. Revelation 2:2-4 ESV

Remember your first love? I sure do. I couldn't spend enough time with him, hung on his every word, believed it all and couldn't wait to introduce my new beau to just *every*one.

For our first love we abandon all, until the excitement dims into the mundane and one day we find ourselves asking the one who gave us shivers to take out the trash and stop hogging the bed. And we wonder how it happened.

We lose freshness and presence. Somehow time, people, and responsibilities took first place.

It can be the same when we experience Jesus for the first time. I remember looking up at *my Love at first sight*—I needed to be shackled! I was reckless with zeal to declare my new love to anyone with ears. The image of my broken life faded into the deep wash of grace. Of course, I had to tell someone—everyone.

Wouldn't you?

I ask you, and I ask me . . . are we still as passionate about our relationship with Christ or do we need to rekindle our first love?

You may have been bruised by life and fallen out of love with the One who abandoned all for you. Or maybe you haven't met yet. I'd love to be matchmaker . . . *wink.*

But I know from experience, if you allow Him to court you, He will bring gifts. Jewels of faith. He will whisper unfailing love into your ear and come on bended knee to ask you to spend the rest of your life with Him.

But watch out! His rival also comes courting and does all he can to rob us of our deep devotion to complicate our relationship with our Betrothed. We get caught up in intellectualizing the Bible instead of receiving just the simple beauty of His love letter.

At the end of the day, and at the end of life, only one relationship will matter. Romance with the Redeemer.

Revisit your sacred moment. And may Jesus restore to you the excitement of first holy glance.

Can you remember the first time Jesus looked into your eyes—your heart?

Worry Knot

Therefore do not be anxious for tomorrow, for tomorrow will care for itself. Each day has enough trouble of its own. Matthew 6:34

Do you ever worry enough to feel knotted up inside? It isn't difficult to court negative feelings in a whirlwind world. We worry about our children, families, jobs, government, economics, rumors and realities of war, contagious diseases, catastrophic weather patterns . . . and a litany of other reasons to angst.

The definition of worry is to "choke or strangle." I guess because it chokes our peace. The Greek root (*merimnao*) means to *divide* . . . in other words, go to pieces. How many do you know falling to pieces?

Often we deceive ourselves and dress worry as concern. The difference is the ability to take action out of concern or identify it as something out of our control (and, you may have noticed, most things are). So then, it's just wasting time and emotion stewing over something we can't fix.

Certainly, I understand there are those who struggle with a medical problem of anxiety, but I'm thinking of those of us who wring our hands with the today and tomorrow *what-ifs.* Before we know it, we allow them to ambush our minds and steal sleep, when worries seem to grow in the dark.

Jesus, the One in control, has a solution. ***Stop it.***

I can share an example of someone who leaves a forever-mark on my heart—my husband, Jeff. He was never one to worry, no matter what the day held before him . . . once an uncertain orphan about tomorrow, and then lost jobs, financial strain, a child born with kidney failure, another son not expected to live following a near-fatal car accident, in wait of the prodigal who left the porch light glowing night after night, and finally a no-hope diagnosis after decades of afflictions . . . and through it all he rested in the grace of today. One of his favorite expressions was a line from an old Irish song: "the cares of tomorrow can wait till this day is done." We listened together the night before he passed away—and I'll hear it forever.

Can you cast the cares of tomorrow on the One who has control over it all?

Trust

Bound to Be Free

And when you stand praying, forgive, if you have anything against anyone, so that your Father also who is in heaven may forgive you your trespasses.
Mark 5:25 ESV

The world is full of people who have not dealt with an old hurt. I've been one of them.

How often have you met someone who tells the same old story a thousand times of the person who offended them a thousand years ago? They rehearse and nurse the grudge until they have the grievance so memorized, you have to wonder how they could ever forget what happened to them. And so they don't.

The root and fruit of bitterness grows into something that tangles us tight. We can all share war stories of the wrong that's been done, or we choose to tell of the victory in how we have broken free from the festering unforgive-ables.

Like the baby elephant tied to a stake from the time he can walk. When he grows into a massive mammal that can uproot trees, he still believes he's bound to the stake he grew up with. He could've broken free long ago when he experienced the power to do so, but he kept himself mentally and habitually bound.

We too can break free from the bitter stake of our past that holds us back from experiencing true freedom. Bitterness is a prison that only we have the key. The key is inside of us.

The story of Joseph (Genesis 25–33) is a beautiful example of letting go of an unwelcomed interruption in life. Thrown into a pit and sold out by jealous brothers, he had plenty of reason to not get over it. While residing with his Egyptian master, Mrs. Potiphar had an eye for the handsome young Joseph, and when he resisted, she insisted . . .and things got ugly. His integrity said no. *No* to her and *no* to bitterness.

Like Joseph, we can allow God to be in charge of our justice. He knew the sovereign God who allows circumstances to carry out the bigger purpose.

When we allow others to affect the course of our lives, we face a decision. Though we can't change the past, we will affect the future by our response. We can fuel bitterness or we can lay our scars before the Healer and ask for the grace to forgive.

Scars tell a story that healing has taken place. Let's celebrate the freedom we have in Christ, who has given the key to unlock the chains of shame, guilt, and bitterness.

Did you drop your keys? Is there something you are holding onto instead?

Unmet Mentors

I seek the quiet place in the morning. There's nothing like my sun porch at 5 a.m. to hear the voice of God above the sound of dawn breaking wide open.

It's my uninterrupted time in the Word of God, before *life* begins. It's also the time I get to spend with an unmet mentor, Lettie Cowman. A woman who lived for nearly a century and continues to live today within her writings, *Streams in the Desert.* With the exception of my Bible, no book has met me as personally and dramatically as this classic devotional.

Years ago, a dear friend gave a copy to me during a fragile time. It not only brought comfort but was also a survival guide to help me through a dark valley. I read it day after day and year after year, and it means as much today as it did then. Each meditation of encouragement recorded in the sacred journal brings me closer to the heart of God.

Out of Mrs. Cowman's experience and heartbreak came a compilation of quotes and inspirational thoughts that helped sustain her throughout her husband's long illness. Written by a woman who knows . . . *really knows.* Despite the

1920s language, I can read and re-read her heart between the antiquated lines and find my own.

Her deep writings became bread and water in the parched places of my life. *A stream in arid times.*

I'm grateful for those who've gone before us, the timeless wisdom preserved on pages by Spirit-driven pens. And I'm grateful for the mentors of today—Max Lucado and Charles Stanley, to name a few.

I'm forever thankful for the one who taught me to study the Bible, Kay Arthur . . . and the one who helped me "break free," Beth Moore. Although there will never be a substitute for my old tattered Bible, how grateful I am for powerful devotions written by Oswald Chambers and Corrie ten Boom, but mostly, the lady who likes to be identified as Mrs. Charles Cowman.

A personal excerpt from her foreword . . .

In the pathway of faith we come to learn that the Lord's thoughts are not our thoughts, nor His ways our ways. Both in the physical and spiritual realm, great pressure means great power! Although circumstances may bring us into the place of death, that need not spell disaster—for if we trust in the Lord and wait patiently, that simply provides the occasion for the display of His almighty power. "Remember His marvelous works that He hath done; His wonders and judgments of His mouth" (Psalm 105:5 KJV).[2]

Who is your favorite unmet mentor?

[2] L. B. Cowman, *Streams in the Desert: 366 Daily Devotional Readings* (Grand Rapids, MI: Zondervan, 1997).

It's a Wonderful Changed Life

For I have come down from heaven, not to do My will, but the will of Him who sent Me. John 6:38

Standing on the edge of a snow-covered iron bridge, George Bailey wishes he had never been born and is ready to end his life in the icy waters below. He has no idea how truly blessed he is until he has an enlightening experience with a loveable apprentice angel by the name of Clarence.

Life stands still for George as he is taken on a journey of his life and sees what it would be like for those whose lives he touched if he hadn't been born. Humbled by the rush of supportive friends to help him in his time of desperation, I see myself and it brings tears to my eyes as I remember so many times when friends embraced our family in times of need.

The final scene has an elated man, grateful for life, running through the streets of Bedford Falls wishing everything and everyone a Merry Christmas. It's easy to relate.

One of our traditions every year is to watch *It's a Wonderful* Life and also the classic tale by Dickens, *A*

Christmas Carol. No matter how familiar I am with the tales, I glean something new every time.

With tight face and tight pockets, Ebenezer Scrooge works his faithful employee Cratchit in the cold of a Christmas Eve candlelight. The ghost of Jacob Marley comes to warn the uncharitable miser that he'll be next to carry the chains if he doesn't repent. Mr. Scrooge spends the night with three spirits who show him what has passed, what is now, and what will come. Standing in the shadow of his own grave, he has a revelation and wakes up as light as a feather and merry as a schoolboy! The best Christmas stories are about changed lives. But do you see a spiritual message in these classics?

Like George's story, what if Jesus had never been born?

There would be a vacant crèche.

What would the world be like if Immanuel hadn't been transported from heaven into a holy womb to come to earth and live among the people and die for every one of them?

The Bible would have ended in Malachi. God's silence.

We would not be able to approach the God of heaven. Our prayers would be wasted breath falling on a distant ear.

The afflicted would remain blind, deaf, and lame. The dead would stay dead.

There would be no tears as we sing "Silent Night," because there was no silent night. There would be no Christmas.

No forgiveness. No hope.

Every holy season reveals more of Jesus and what He has done in my life. I don't need a George Bailey moment to realize that without Him I would still be on the same destructive path. Let us remember together, it's a wonderful-changed life . . . because Jesus came into it.

How would your life be different if Jesus had never been born? How would the lives you have touched been different without you?

The One We Seek Is Not Hiding

I love those who love Me; and those who diligently seek Me will find Me. Proverbs 8:17

In the scrapbook of my mind, I can still see my children scrambling to search for friends while playing the game of Hide and Seek. Lifting lids, checking dark corners, sneaking behind the barn, looking up in the apple tree, diligently trying to find the one who was hiding. Sometimes in frustration they would walk away from the game before finding the one who was hidden. Sounds a bit antiquated, when kids played outside, I know, but this was a time of jacks, stickball, and marbles.

Many of us are on the same wearisome hunt. Looking for God somewhere in the midst of countless negative stuff of today. So, where is He hiding?

The other day I set out on a deliberate God hunt just to discover the many ways He was right in view. I saw Him behind the eyes of one loving friend who gave a gift of rest to another. I heard Him in the sounds of the morning perched on branches above my path. A God-scent surrounded me in the handspun balsam and cedar limbs I walked beside. And then I witnessed His obvious touch in the helping hand extended to the one who fell. There, in unveiled senses, was no place He could remain hidden.

The Father is not one who hides from the seeker. Where have you looked for Him today?

Divine Un-Coincidence

And your ears shall hear a word behind you, saying, "This is the way, walk in it." Isaiah 30:21 ESV

Do you care what time it is in Uganda? I never thought much of the time zone on the far side of the globe until my eighteen-year-old granddaughter left for the pearl of Africa. In spite of living in an era of instant communication, she had limited opportunity to connect home because of the location. It didn't help that the little exchange we had with her was to find that she and part of the missions team had contracted malaria.

Awakened in the night to pray, I wondered what she was doing in this African moment . . . sleeping or thinking of home.

Our daughter, the missionary mom, continued to check her phone but didn't hear from her until one restless night when she got up in the exact Holy Spirit moment to check Facebook, and there was Taleh. Five minutes later would have been five minutes too late.

Mr. Webster defines a *coincidence* as "the occurrence of events that happen at the same time by accident but seem to have some connection."[3] If I ever decide to write a dictionary, my definition will read, ***"when mercy moments collide perfectly."***

Coincidence and sovereignty don't mix. There is only the scattering of miracles from the almighty keeper of time and space, the One who wound the first clock.

Once on an October night in 2000, husband Jeff was carving in his workshop on the lower level of our home. I was busy, two floors above in my sewing room. We both finished our work at the same time and joined each other in front of the fireplace. Within ten minutes of coming together in the living room, he suffered a massive heart attack. I was there in the CPR moment (which just has to mean *continuous-prayer-regardless*), and after an arduous journey, he lived.

Twice upon a time, on another October night, this time in 2002, I was awakened from sleep at 3 a.m. to pray for a son who didn't come home. Within a half hour, while I was pleading on knees, a hospital chaplain called to say our son had been in a near-fatal car accident and may not live. He was

---

[3] *Merriam-Webster Online.* Accessed August 11. 2016. http://www.merriam-webster.com/dictionary/coincidence

so damaged he could only be identified as John Doe, and after another arduous journey, he lived.

Oh, and the never-can-forget January afternoon in 1979. Pregnant with our fourth child, a month before due, with no symptoms of labor and only a holy stir to leave for the hospital in the middle of a snow storm . . . after delivery, I was told that my son was only a half hour from stillbirth. Thirty minutes later would have been too late. When the doctor asked how I knew to get to the hospital in that moment, I think God answered for me. And after still yet another arduous journey, he lived.

We can't make our own coincidences happen. Try. Instead we must simply meditate on the divines that touch our lives, sometime elusive, sometimes clear.

What is your divine un-coincidence?

Chatting with Your Soul

Bless the LORD, O my soul, and all that is within me.
Psalm 103:1

Would you believe you are able to make a difference in your emotional, spiritual, and physical well-being by talking to yourself?

The psaltery journal of David—penned in palaces, caves, and shepherd fields—reminds us how he strengthened himself in the words of the Lord. When his soul was downcast, he chatted with his inner breath.

We don't know what kind of day he was having when he jotted down Psalm 103, but he sounded fairly overwhelmed with life. Probably like us.

Think about your day or past week(s) and ask yourself how any of the overwhelming times you may have experienced could have been different if you reversed the negative by affirming with a positive? It may not change the situation, but it should change the way you deal with it.

I've worked in a doctor's office for nearly twenty years, and during that time I've been surrounded by those battling health and death, family and financial struggle, with worried hearts that believe a pill will mend it all.

We need hope. We need encouragement. The word *hope* means confident expectation and the word *encouragement* means to urge forward. We can urge ourselves (and others) forward with a positive attitude.

When self tells you you'll never get passed this because it's all there is, allow the counsel of your soul to turn a deaf ear.

If you believe you can't do something—you won't.

So, when faith dims, make Psalm 103 your prayer . . . aloud. Speak the Word of God over your health, your circumstances, your children, and your life.

"Bless and affectionately praise the LORD, O my soul, and do not forget any of His benefits. Who forgives all your sins, who heals all your diseases; who redeems your life from the pit, who crowns you [lavishly] with loving kindness and tender mercy; who satisfies your years with good things so that your youth is renewed like the [soaring] eagle" (Psalm 103:2–5 AMP).

So, how do you think David got from the place of I-think-I-can to I-*know*-I-can, or I-think-God-can to I-*know*-God-can? And how can we?

He experienced a lot of life in his shepherd-to-a-king days, filled with fear, mistakes, and mourning, and he got through by coaching his soul and remembering the goodness and greatness of God.

So rehearse the Psalm 103 promises—he forgives, heals, redeems, surrounds, and contents us with good. It will shout loud over the voice of despair.

So self, echo to soul that today some good things will happen.

And record them here . . .

Hope

Waiting at the Well

The water that I give him will become in him a well of water springing up to eternal life. John 4:14

What do we do with a lifetime of bad choices? We can quit and say that's all there is, but if we do that we just made another bad choice.

It doesn't have to be the ending to our story.

In the fourth chapter of the book of John, there are forty-two verses devoted to an unnamed Samaritan woman who met the Savior face-to-face and was changed forever. The story records the longest dialogue Jesus has with anyone in the Gospels. And this chat happened to be with a woman that no Jewish man would be caught talking with.

Jesus traveled out of His way on a personal mission to seek this one living in a despised land. Back in the day, Jews and Samaritans were rivals and didn't mingle.

Tired and thirsty, He waits in the shade of Jacob's Well in the heat of the day. Ordinarily, women came to the wells at sunset, but this particular lady came at an appointed time. Shunned for her lifestyle, the outcast woman came to draw water at noon to avoid the glances and gossip of the villagers. You see, Ms. Samaritan had been a Mrs. many times, and at the time was a Ms. living like a Mrs.

For the first time, the rejected woman sees compassion in the eyes of a Man. He asks for a drink, and she is confused that He would consider drinking from the same vessel as an ostracized Samaritan.

The only Man who can change the life of the woman at the well gazes behind her eyes into the well of her soul. They talked about the barriers of culture, religion, and race, but then got to the important part, when mercy met sin. He told her who she was. And who He was.

Deep hurt, lies, and sin kept her from the truth of knowing who God is. *Until now*. At a well He unveils His identity as the true Messiah. In the drought of her spirit, she is eternally quenched with the Living Water.

We are all thirsty for truth and crave something greater. Her story is a reminder that there is a "well of meeting" in the dry places of life where a merciful Father is waiting to touch us to permanently heal the deep.

The unlikely candidate was used to advance the gospel in a region where it had not been heard. She enthusiastically told of her new passion, Jesus the Messiah, who changed her life in a holy moment.

Because of this life-changing encounter, she not only experienced salvation but many others also came to believe.

Do you remember when Jesus went out of His way to meet you? What was your response?

Conflict Declawed

There is one who speaks rashly like the thrusts of a sword, but the tongue of the wise brings healing. Proverbs 12:18

Do you have trouble dealing with tension in your circles? How about unkind words?

We all remember the *sticks and stones will break your bones but words will never hurt you* days of grade school. Secrets, whispers, tale-bearing. Things left in the dust of history spoken out only to recycle pain. And then the times we wore our judge's robe and asked, "Do you remember what she did?" and passed down a lifelong sentence to Susie.

It happened to me, to my daughter, also to my granddaughters, and probably you and yours. We can all share incidents when another girl deliberately wounded us. Like me, you were probably tempted to wound right back. Or, maybe we were the one who wounded first.

Sadly, the church is not exempt from tension and conflict. It's happened to ladies down through time. I think of the first century catfight when the apostle Paul mediated between two squabbling women greatly affecting the unity of the church in Philippi. The only time they show up in Scripture is recording their dispute. It was important enough for Paul to write down because it caused division in the body of Christ. He says in Philippians 4:2, "I urge Euodia and I urge Syntyche to live in harmony in the Lord."

Women are relational. I am grateful for my longtime friends since childhood who no others could replace, and for forever friendships I've met along the way with women of faith who have kept me from sinking or wanting to jump ship in my adult life.

A friend's concern and counsel can change our day . . . our lives. Women need women.

We can learn from the gracious example of Hannah. She was married to Elkanah, who had another wife. Her rival was Peninnah (the fertile wife), who brought her to tears daily by flaunting her children before the barren Hannah. She could respond in bitterness to the provoking Peninnah or cry her heart out to her Father in heaven. She chose the latter and took the matter to God.

From the depth of her heart she cried out to her Lord. Grief and tears mounted up until they burst into one of the most passionate prayers recorded in Scripture (1 Samuel 2:1–10).

Even when misunderstood by the temple priest who accused her of being filled with wine as she prayed so fervently, so silently she cried out rather than lashing out. Her response was, "No . . . I am a woman oppressed in spirit. . . . I have poured out my soul to the LORD." Eli then blessed her.

Love spreads its mantle over those who choose God's ways, and Hannah birthed a prophet! Samuel, the son dedicated and offered to the good care of God.

Our words can be a blessing or a landmine. Is God allowing a Peninnah into your life? Burst into prayer, for He is ready to birth something in you!

Beloved

I end with a special entry from my journal that I wrote after my husband's memorial celebration this past February. In remembrance of the one who helped me gather . . . pieces of life.

I whispered a final good-bye to my beloved last Friday on a windy cemetery hill . . . temporarily. But *Because He Lives,* I can face tomorrow and have the blessed assurance I'll see him again, and forever.

Our Pastor John has a way of eulogizing a life with a gospel-word. The word chosen for Jeff is *beloved.* However, Jeff may not have always agreed the word to be fitting. Sometimes the weight of our story is too much to read.

Our Girard brother Jon, the wordsmith, eulogizes a life by taking us through the dark tunnels of Jeff's solitude and walking us through the orphan halls of Girard to get a deeper glimpse of who he was and who he became. *Beloved.*

Our son-in-law, Scott, and oldest grandson, Japheth, create a resting place with hands and heart, and the casket blesses the people. *Beloved.*

Grandchildren sing of a circle that will be unbroken even after we fly away, and sons and daughters testify of a man who left a loving mark upon their lives. *Beloved.*

And so, when we review our life story, can we really believe that we have been beloved? Could Jeff, although life hit hard from the beginning and until the end when a death sentence seemingly came one letter at a time? Yes.

We can be assured of the Father's kind attention, no matter how it appears to others. And we can be sure there is a loving mystery that uses it all to draw us to the deep place of His presence. So, Pastor John chose well—the title of Jeff's memorial story. It's the same title of mine, and yours.

Beloved.

And that is why I know that my beloved dwells between the shoulders of the Father, where the chosen is no longer a fatherless boy. He is held tight and secure in His presence.

May the beloved of the Lord dwell in security by Him, who shields him all the day, and he dwells between His shoulders. Deuteronomy 33:12

Notes

Are you living your questions or your answers?

Verna loves to tell the story – and encourage women one story at a time.

This one woman's story will help you discover a faith that cannot be shattered by brokenness and how you, too, can walk through and not around adversity in *Crumbs Along the Broken Path.*

She is available to speak at your women's event.

Please contact:
gvbowman@comcast.net
www.vernabowman.com

Made in the USA
Middletown, DE
23 September 2016